# PRAYERS
FOR
ISRAEL

# PRAYERS
## FOR
# ISRAEL

NEW AND ANCIENT PRAYERS BASED ON
PALMS, SACRED WRITINGS,
AND TEACHINGS OF HASIDIC MASTERS

---

## RABBI YONAH BOOKSTEIN

---

Stone Oak Publishing • Los Angeles

Prayers for Israel

Copyright ©2012 by Yonah Bookstein.

rabbiyonah.com | @rabbiyonah

---

All rights reserved. Printed in the United States of America. No part of this book may be used or reproduced in any manner whatsoever without written permission except in the case of brief quotations embodied in critical articles and reviews. For information contact Stone Oak Publishing: ybookstein@yahoo.com

---

First Edition September 2012

www.prayersforisrael.com

---

ISBN-10: 1477516743

BISAC: Religion / Prayerbooks / General

*For Rabbi Chaskel Besser Z"L and Rabbi Shlomo Carlebach Z"L, of blessed memory, who loved Israel with all their soul and might. The light, joy, and wisdom they revealed continue to illuminate the world.*

# CONTENTS

**Acknowledgements** ............................................................. 1

**Introduction** ..................................................................... 5

**Chapter One:** The Holiness of Israel ............................ 13
    Israel the Holiness of the World ............................. 14
    Holiness Begins with the Holy Temple ............ 16
    Why do Jews Have a Claim to Israel? .................. 17
    What is the Holiness of Israel? ............................... 18

**Chapter Two:** Everyday Prayers .................................... 19
    Asking for our Prayers to be Heard ..................... 20
    Oneness of God ............................................................ 21
    Grant Us Salvation ..................................................... 22
    In-gathering of Exiles ................................................ 23
    Against Detractors and Persecutors ..................... 25
    For the Righteous ....................................................... 26
    Rebuilding Jerusalem ................................................ 27

Prayer for the State of Israel ................................. 28
Coming of the Messiah ....................................... 30
Accept our Prayers ............................................. 32
Prayer for Peace ................................................. 33
A Personal Prayer .............................................. 34
Prayer for our Brothers and Sister in Distress ..... 35

**Chapter Three:** Daily Prayers for Israel's Protection .. 37
Your Sheltering Peace ........................................ 39
Remember Your Promise ................................... 40
The Great Protector ........................................... 41
Stop the Evil Plans ............................................ 42
Guardian of Israel ............................................. 43
Prayer for Israel's Soldiers .................................. 44
Prayers for Soldiers in Captivity ......................... 45
Psalm 144 .......................................................... 46

**Chapter Four:** Daily Psalms For Israel ..................... 49
Psalm 20 ........................................................... 50
Psalm 83 ........................................................... 52

Psalm 121 .................................................................... 54
Psalm 130 .................................................................... 55
Psalm 142 .................................................................... 56

**Chapter Five:** Meditations ............................................... 57
- Hear My Prayers ........................................................ 59
- We may Sing to You .................................................. 60
- Restore Our Prestige ................................................. 61
- Bring Us To Your Holy Land ................................... 62

**Chapter Six:** Prayers for Jerusalem ................................ 65
- Service of the Heart .................................................. 66
- Beauty ......................................................................... 67
- Psalm 122 ................................................................... 68
- Blessed is Jerusalem the Home of Prayer ............ 69
- Next Year in Jerusalem ............................................ 70
- Psalm 137 ................................................................... 71

**Chapter Seven:** Prayers for Times of Crisis ................. 73
- Awakening God's Compassion ............................... 74

Prayer for Captives .................................................. 75
Prayer for Zion and Jerusalem ................................ 75
How Long Must There be Weeping? ..................... 76
Psalm for Great Crisis – Psalm 59 .......................... 77
Save me from my Enemies ....................................... 77
Prayers for Rain ......................................................... 80
Creator of the Universe Answer our Prayers .......... 81
Answer Us – A Prayer for Rain ............................... 83

# About This Book ..................................................... 85

# How To Use This Book ......................................... 89

# Bibliography ............................................................. 99

# Endnotes .................................................................. 103

# About the Author .................................................. 111

# Acknowledgements

*"Give thanks and praise to the Lord."*
— BOB MARLEY

# ACKNOWLEDGEMENTS

I would like to thank my teachers of blessed memory, Rabbi Chaskel Besser and Rabbi Shlomo Carlebach, who taught me to pray and to love Judaism. The world still weeps over the loss of these two giants of Jewish learning, devoted servants of God, defenders of the Jewish people, and lovers of Israel.

My deepest gratitude to Rabbis Shraga Feival Zimmerman, Mati Kos, Shaya Karlinski, and Yehudah Ferris for their support and guidance that help me each day to fulfill God's will.

I am grateful to Rabbi Avraham Greenbaum for his eloquent translations of Reb Nosson's prayers, some of which I have included in this book. The power of praying in English opened up a new world of prayer. If not for many months of prayer with this translation, I doubt that I would have felt the ability to author a contemporary book of prayers.

Thank you to my book editor Seth Abelson for your time, patience, and energy. To my designer Rebecca Ludlam and Lisa Klug for your help.

Thank you to my father Marvin, of blessed memory, and my mother Denah, who first taught me to love and appreciate Israel, and to my ancestors and cousins who helped defend and support Israel through wars and crisis.

My deepest gratitude to my wife Rachel who allowed me time to write and reviewed every word of this book. Her editing and suggestions were invaluable. Rachel helped me to transform the Psalms into contemporary English, which will help everyone using this book. Without her encouragement this would have never come to fruition.

Lastly, I am thankful to God. I am humbled and grateful for the opportunity to write and organize these prayers before You. Thank You for the infinite blessings which You bestow upon me and my family. Thank You for inspiring me each day to serve You in joy and good health.

*"You must pray for everything."*
— REBBE NACHMAN

# ❧INTRODUCTION

> *"We usually think of prayer as asking God for something. But it is much more than that. The deepest depth of prayer is that we are making a connection. Through the simple act of praying, just in itself, we connect ourselves so closely with God."*
>
> — RABBI SHLOMO CARLEBACH [01]

## INTRODUCTION

If you picked up this book chances are that you feel, as I do, that prayer can do immeasurable good in the world. The book you are holding is the first book of prayers compiled in English about and for Israel. No such book has ever existed. Here you will find ancient Jewish prayers, selections of King David's Psalms, other sacred writings, and teachings of Hasidic masters. It contains heartfelt prayers that give voice to our hopes, concerns, and faith. This is a new chapter in the campaign for Israel's safety and well-being that I hope will make praying for Israel a regular part of people's lives. This book is an ecumenical book for those who love Israel and want a new and powerful tool to advocate for Israel's peace and wellbeing.

Lovers of Israel spend time and resources defending Israel, but in my experience I see that not enough time is set aside to pray for Israel. There are times when we are so wrapped up in standing for Israel in the public sphere, that we let this powerful weapon fall into disuse. Yet, prayer is the most powerful tool at our disposal to help heal what is broken, to protect what is vulnerable, and overcome what is challenging. The opportunity for prayer is always with us. Thought at times it is not easy to pour out our feelings and fears to the Creator, it is much easier when we have words to attach our feelings.

Many Synagogues and Temples include a prayer for Israel during their services. Some people recite Psalms regularly for Israel's safety and security. Some large Christian groups include prayers for Israel in their services and have formed virtual prayer groups and websites in order to include Israel in their daily prayers. There are Christian and Jewish groups that send out email blasts reminding people to pray for Israel regularly. In addition, many missions to Israel include prayer sessions in their itinerary.

However, the average person who cares about Israel is not praying every day for Israel. Why? One answer is that prayer is abstract. There is no tangible evidence of our prayer being even be received, no email from on high. If that weren't enough to challenge us, we don't get an immediate answer to our requests. Rest assured every prayer is heard. As Rebbe Nachman of Breslov taught, "You must believe that God listens and pays attention to every word of prayer, so that a single word is not lost."

Another one of the reasons that we are not praying everyday for Israel, is we don't see that Israel's situation is truly dire. When things get bad, and our beloved Holy Land is under attack, and the news is filled with images of war and destruction — then we start praying. Perhaps we don't even know the prayers and our lips don't know what words to say, but we ask God for mercy and intervention. We make promises to God and deals with God. As when a friend or loved one is in intensive care we say, "God if you just heal them I promise to..." We generally keep prayer as a weapon of last resort.

We often can't find the words to express our most heartfelt yearnings, which is why prayer books are so helpful. We know in our hearts what we want to say, but sometimes it's hard to open up the conversation. My goal is that this book will help keep open the lines of communication between God and us in relation to the

Land of Israel. I want it to be used to strengthen our ability to pray, to recognize that prayer, as speech and song, is a powerful form of spiritual activism. When things are good for Israel, we can give thanks and offer blessings, and when things are not good, we have an established channel, and an organized group of prayers to use when we speak to God and ask God to intercede.

In addition to keeping open the lines of communication, Israel truly needs our prayers every day. Just as organizations that fight for Israel, defend Israel, care for Israel, support Israel, and feed Israel need contributions of time and resources, so too does the collective prayer for Israel need all of our voices. Our contribution of time, and resources towards the safety and wellbeing of Israel are essential. So too is the amazing work of activists and volunteers caring for daily needs of Israel. Our prayers are also an essential part of the equation. When Israelis know that others are praying for them, they are encouraged and supported in their struggle and their spiritual practice.

As a rabbi I am often asked to pray for people. Nowhere does it say that a layperson's prayers don't work. Yet, there is something ingrained in our society that transcends cultural and religious affiliation where people feel comforted if they believe that a clergyperson is praying for them. The truth is that the prayers of each person, in any language, are beloved to God.

When it comes to Israel and the dawning of an age promised by the prophets more than 2,000 years ago, we need to undo the cultural myth that only certain people hold the key to prayer. Israel needs rabbis and priests praying, but what Israel needs most is each one of us praying for its peace and security.

Our prayers are not only for Israel's security — they are also for Israel's redemption. Tied so closely together, we pray for the Messianic era when Israel will be delivered from its enemies, peace will reign, and a just and good society will welcome the Messiah. Yet, we too can become weary of this anticipation. We have waited so long, that praying for the redemption, praying for salvation, praying for the Messiah, can become tiring, sometimes even an afterthought.

We cannot tarry nor can we be quiet in our devotion to the coming redemption. As the founder of the Hasidic movement, the Ba'al Shem Tov said, 'One must serve God in all of one's ways, so one must anticipate the redemption in all one's ways.

If we really believe that Israel is the Holy Land, that the welfare and safety of the Land of Israel is paramount to our faith, then we cannot sit idly by. In addition to defending Israel in the public arena, we must urgently raise our voices in prayer. We need to bring our requests directly before God, and dedicate time, devotion, and willpower to our worship. Through increasing our prayers for Israel, this will also give us strength to continue working for peace and security and defending Israel.[02]

We will raise our voices in prayer!

We will devote time each day praying for Israel's well being with mediations, psalms, personal prayers, and words from sages.

We must contribute our time and prayers to safeguard Israel and to facilitate the redemption.

# CHAPTER 1
# THE HOLINESS OF ISRAEL

*"There is a Midrash that states that after the Messiah comes, the holiness within the Holy of Holies will expand to the whole Temple, the holiness of the Temple will spread to all Jerusalem, the holiness of Jerusalem will spread out to all of Israel and the holiness of Israel will encompass the entire world."*

— BASED ON PESIKTA RABBATI, SHABBAT V'ROSH CHODESH 2 [03]

*Why do we pray for Israel? There are many reasons. One powerful reason is because Israel is the most powerful source of holiness for the world. Rabbi Shlomo Carlebach spoke about this beautiful idea in the name of Rebbe Nachman of Breslov. His words and teaching are retold below as adapted by Dr. Zvi Ritchei.*

## ISRAEL THE HOLINESS OF THE WORLD

Everything in the world has a certain level of holiness. When I walk on the street and I give a poor man a dollar, it is holy, when I wake up in the morning and praise God — it is holy. Whatever I do is holy, but it is only part of holiness. But there is something that is the headquarters for holiness. Whatever holiness there is in the world is included there. This is the Holy Land, this is what the land of Israel is all about.

The land of Israel encompasses all holiness. And as I speak all the time about Jerusalem, people ask me, "Why are you talking so much about Jerusalem? Bombay is also Holy, Amsterdam is Holy." It's true; every city has a certain holiness, because if it were completely devoid of holiness it would cease to exist. There may be bad things, but there has to be something holy, otherwise it would cease to exist. I'm not trying to put them down, they are holy, but the Land of Israel is something else. The Land of Israel is the house of all the holiness.

Imagine if you would take all the holiness wherever it is; all of the commandments, all the good deeds, all the cities, all the houses, and you would put it all in one place. That is what the land of Israel is all about.

# Holiness Begins with the Holy Temple

The world always thinks that since the Land of Israel is holy, so Jerusalem is more holy because it is the capital, and the Holy Temple is even more holy than Jerusalem because we pray towards it every day. But really, it is the other way around. The great sages tell us [Maimonides] that the holiness of the land of Israel begins with the Holy Temple, this is the center of the world. The center of the world is the Holy Temple, which houses the holy of holies, and Jerusalem is holy because it is close to the Holy Temple, and the Land of Israel is holy because of Jerusalem. So everything, all of holiness, begins in Jerusalem, in the Holy Temple.

## Why do Jews Have a Claim to Israel?

Rebbe Nachman says: Where does our claim to Israel come from? The Talmud and Rashi say; "Why did God tell us the story of creation? The Torah is actually a book of laws, why did God tell us the story of Creation? Because some day the world will say, 'What are you doing in Israel?' and we will answer them, 'God created the world, He gave Israel to us.' Our claim on Israel is on the level of creation, based on the goodness of God, and not because we deserve it."

# What is the Holiness of Israel?

And Rebbe Nachman says, "What is the holiness of Israel, of the Holy Land? The holiness of the Land of Israel is the holy thing that you don't give up." This is the secret of the Holy Land. Because the Holy Land is not giving up — I never give up, because God wants to give it to me. It has nothing to do with whether we deserve it or not. It is our birthright from the time God gave it to our ancestors.

# Chapter 2

## Everyday Prayers

*"Blessed are You who has sanctified us with Your commandments and obliged us to be engaged with the words of Your Holy words."*

— BASED ON THE MORNING BLESSINGS

*The ancient sages taught that by establishing a set time for prayer we create a meeting with God. God, as it were, waits to hear from us at this appointed time, and when we miss it, God wonders what happened to us.*

## Asking for our Prayers to be Heard

Creator of the Universe, God of our ancestors, hear the words of our prayers with kindness, prepare our hearts so that we may concentrate on our prayers and thoughts. Put the right words in our mouths that You may hear our prayers. Strengthen our connection and love for You. Make all our prayers be pleasant for You. You alone know the true will of our hearts. Hear our prayers with an open hand and a generous heart. Amen.

## Oneness of God

God of Abraham and Sarah, who taught the world about Your oneness, show us a holy path so we may live better lives, worship only You, and devote ourselves to uncovering the sparks of Godliness in everyone and on the Oneness of your existence.[04]

## Grant Us Salvation

Compassionate One, see our affliction and our broken hearts. See how this hatred for Israel we see every day lowers our spirits, induces stress, causes pain in our chests. See our tears and the anguish we suffer from this injustice. See the malicious portrayal of Israel. See the world ignore our testimony, malign our cause, call Zionism a lie, and cast vicious claims against Israel. Influence the many, who remain in doubt, for whom else will they listen to? Though we don't deserve Your intervention on our merits alone, redeem us from this hatred for Your sake. Though we are often ungrateful and far from perfect, plead our case to the world, for we don't know how. You are the only true redeemer. You can redeem us, and Israel, and the entire world. Blessed are You the redeemer of Israel.[05]

## In-gathering of Exiles

God, don't wait any longer for we are impatient. Show us the end of these 2,000 years of waiting. Lift up our weary spirits. Fulfill your promise today. Gather the dispersed Jewish people who have spread to four corners of the Earth. Gather those who are spiritually distant. Gather those who have forgotten or never knew who they are.

You show us the signs of this impending redemption with the flowering of the hills of Israel, and the bountiful harvest. Look and see what I see — the hills and plains and valleys of Israel blooming; the barren sand turned to soil; the fertile land overflowing with ripe fruit and fragrant honey. Make this the appointed time. Sound the great shofar for the redemption. Raise the banner of freedom; raise the banner of liberation; raise the banner of justice; gather us today from the ends of the Earth. Resist being dissuaded by our narrow vision because deep down we know Israel is our spiritual home. You know because You engraved it on our hearts. Our souls yearn for home. Redeem Your people. Why make us wait any longer?

Blessed are You, who gathers together the dispersed People of Israel.[06]

## Against Detractors and Persecutors

Save us God from the sadness we carry each day as Israel is delegitimized, falsely accused, from those who declare Israel the root and cause of all evil. Heal our hearts, which are battered and bruised by the defamers of Your land and the People of Israel. Bring clarity to those who don't know Israel, and are uneducated and unaware. Offer no rest for those who spread falsehoods, rumors, and accusations about the Jewish people and Your land. Turn their hearts. Inspire them to repent and abandon their ways. Give them opportunities to repent. Show them righteous people who will inspire them to change their minds. Make those who spread lies become spokesman for truth. Break their influence so their false words wither and perish. Restore the prestige and influence of the righteous among us. Blessed are You who breaks Israel's enemies and humbles the sinners. [07]

## CHAPTER TWO

# FOR THE RIGHTEOUS

Bless the righteous and the devout that defend the Land of Israel with their souls and their might. Protect them from spiritual and physical harm. Guard them under Your sheltering wings, and give them courage to withstand the insults, abuse, and the mockery they suffer for defending Israel. Provide strength for the righteous ones who stand in support of Israel, tirelessly declaring their love for Israel against the detractors. Inspire us God to be among those who stand by Israel. Guide us so we may know where our efforts are needed. Grant us the wisdom to answer those who slander Israel or are ignorant, and grant us the patience not to follow the path of anger. Help Your defenders to live peacefully, to remain devout, and avoid despair, disillusionment, and cynicism. Reward those who sincerely believe in Your name and Your People of Israel. Put our lot with them forever, and we will not feel ashamed, for we trust in You. Blessed are You, Mainstay and Assurance of the righteous.[08]

## Rebuilding Jerusalem

Return with compassion to Jerusalem, Your Holy City. Protect it from harm, division, plunder and strife. Guard the City of Peace, the spiritual center of the world. Guard the gates of the eternal capital of Israel where Solomon's Temple stood and prophets prophesied. Let the joyous voices of the bridegroom and bride be heard in the surrounding hills. Fill the streets with visitors and pilgrims from the four corners of the Earth. Provide sustenance for those who dwell in Jerusalem. Bless this place where Heaven meets Earth, where Abraham's hand was stilled, where Jacob dreamed, where David danced, and Jeremiah cried. Rebuild Jerusalem in our days as the eternal home for those who love You and call out Your name. Restore the throne of David. Bring peace to Jerusalem and bless those who love You with peace. Show us the day when the Redeemer will come to Zion through the Golden Gate. Unify this city of dreamers with your love and all of Jerusalem will rejoice as one. Blessed are you God, Builder of Jerusalem.[09]

## Prayer for the State of Israel

Heavenly Creator, Israel's Rock and Redeemer, bless the State of Israel, the first flowering of the Redemption. Shield it under wings of Your loving-kindness and spread over it the Tabernacle of Your peace. Send Your light and truth to its leaders, ministers, and counselors, and direct them with good counsel before You. Strengthen the hands of the defenders of our Holy Land; grant them deliverance, our God, and crown them with the crown of victory. Grant peace in the land and everlasting joy to its inhabitants.

As for our brothers and sisters, the whole House of Israel, remember them in all the lands of our dispersion, and swiftly lead us upright to Zion Your city, and Jerusalem Your dwelling place, as it is written in the Torah of Moses Your servant (Deut. 30): "Even if you are scattered to the furthest most lands under the heavens, from there God will gather you and take you back. God will bring you to the land your ancestors possessed and you will possess it; and God will make you more prosperous and numerous than your ancestors. Then God will open up your hearts and the heart of your descendants to love the Lord Your God with all your heart and with all your soul, that you may live."

Unite our hearts to love and revere Your name and observe all the words of Your teachings, and swiftly send us Your righteous anointed one of the House of David, to redeem those who long for Your salvation.

Appear in Your glorious majesty over all the dwellers of the Earth, and let all who breathe declare: The Creator, the God of Israel is our Ruler and God's sovereignty has dominion over all. Amen Selah.[10]

## CHAPTER TWO

# COMING OF THE MESSIAH

[11]We believe with complete faith in the coming of the Messiah, and if our Redeemer shall tarry we shall impatiently each day. Please fulfill the words of the prophet, "Then God will comfort Zion and all of the desolate ruins." Turn an empty wilderness into the Garden of Eden, and the barren desert into the Garden of God. Fill the land with joy, gladness and prayers of thanksgiving, and the air with the sound of harmonious song.[12]

Show us a path to follow and a way to live our lives in order to hasten the redemption and restore the throne of David in Jerusalem. We want to fulfill the unique mission You have given each of us. Reveal to us this holy task, and we will not rest. Help us to perform more good deeds to tip the scales in our favor.

Without Your redemption we are like a withered tree needing nourishment so it may flourish once again.

Cause a blossom to sprout from the stem of Jesse, and a branch to grow from his roots. And rest upon him Your spirit.[13] Bring the offspring of your loyal servant David to Jerusalem, make him flourish and enhance his influence through Your salvation. We hope and pray for Your salvation with each breath. Blessed are You who causes the hope of salvation to flourish.

## Accept our Prayers

Hear our voice, God. Show pity and be compassionate to us. Accept with grace and favor our prayers. Don't turn us away empty handed. Listen with kindness to the prayers of Your people Israel and the prayers of those who love Israel. Listen as we pray each and every day for Israel, for its well-being and safety, and for Israel to flourish like a date palm in the desert. Send healing to those who are sick so they too can pray for Israel's redemption and follow Your teachings. Provide our families with sustenance so that we may serve You. Be concerned for both our big and small requests. Redeem us, save us, show us compassion so that we may experience Your guiding presence in our lives and the lives of our families. Fulfill the words of Your prophets, "I will bring them to My Holy Mountain and they will rejoice in My house of prayer. For My house shall be called a House of Prayer for all people."[14] Hear with favor the earnest prayers of all people who love the People of Israel. Blessed are You who hears prayers with compassion.[15]

## Prayer for Peace

God please bring peace, goodness, blessing, graciousness, kindness, and compassion to us, to the Nation of Israel, and to all of Your children. Shine Your divine light upon us as a blessing of peace and unity. Bless us with peace of mind so we will not be swayed by negativity, and keep our spirits positive so that we may serve You in peace. Bring peace between those who love You, bring unity and cooperation to those who stand with Israel. Forgive our attitudes and territorialism that impeded our efforts. Overlook our failure to work together. Bless Israel in every season and in every hour with Your peace. Blessed are You Who blesses Israel with peace.[16]

## CHAPTER TWO

# A Personal Prayer

God please find favor with the expressions of my mouth and the thoughts of my heart for Your are my Rock, and my Redeemer. Guard my tongue from evil and my lips from speaking deceitfully. Keep me silent to those who curse me, and remove my egoism so that I may be humble. Open my heart to Your teaching so my soul will pursue Your commandments. Open my heart to humanity, so I may see everyone as being created in Your image. Disrupt the plans of those that design evil against me, and nullify their influence. Act for Your name's sake; Act for Your sanctity's sake, Act for Your Teachings sake. Give rest to Your beloved ones. Save me from worry and distress and respond to me. May the expressions of my mouth and the thoughts of my heart find favor before You God my Rock and my Redeemer. God who makes peace in the heavens make peace upon us, and upon all Israel. Amen.[17]

## Prayer for our Brothers and Sisters in Distress

Our brothers and sisters, and anyone from the family of Israel, who have been caught in danger or captivity, may God be compassionate to them, take them speedily from anguish to relief, from darkness to light, from oppression to redemption right now. And let us say Amen.[18]

# Chapter 3

## Prayers for Israel's Protection

*"As long as in the heart, within, a Jewish soul still yearns. And onward towards the ends of the east, an eye still gazes to Zion. Our hope is not yet lost, the hope of two thousand years. To be a free people in our land, the land of Zion and Jerusalem."*

— HATIKVAH

*Israel is under attack every day of the year. From the missiles that rain down from Gaza or Lebanon, and terrorists who plot evil plans, to cyber-warfare and boycotts, Israel is under constant threat. These prayers ask God to protect Israel and her defenders everyday.*

*As well, the freedom of the People of Israel to dwell securely in the Holy Land comes with a price. Soldiers stand in harm's way from Lebanon to the desert, from Gaza to the Jordan Valley. They patrol the skies and the sea. They watch the borders for intruders. They prepare and train every day to answer the call, should it come, to defend the Homeland. After army service it doesn't end. Each soldier remains on reserve duty, called up every year for army duty.*

*It is incumbent on those who love Israel and the Land of Israel to pray for their safety and wellbeing, that they be protected and kept from harm's way. Some of these prayers are normally recited with a congregation on the Sabbath, but can be recited anytime by a person praying alone or with a group.*

## Your Sheltering Peace

God, our shield and protector, guard Israel today and everyday from missiles and rockets. Shield Israel from attacks and foil the plans of those that seek to do Israel harm. Make their bombs fall from the sky missing their targets. Please guide and protect those who defend Israel's skies. Help them perform their duty and mission with accuracy and effectiveness. Create a heavenly shield to shelter Israel's cities, villages, schools, and homes from this terror. Spread over Israel the wings of Your sheltering peace. Amen.

## Remember Your Promise

Remember, God, Your compassion and loving-kindness, for they are everlasting.

Remember Your congregation Israel, the one that you acquired long ago, the tribe that Your redeemed, this Mount Zion that You have dwelt in.

Remember, God, Your fondness for Jerusalem; do not ever forget Your love of Zion. Rise up and have compassion for Zion, for now it is right to be gracious, for the time has come.

Remember, God, the promise you made to Abraham, Isaac, and Jacob, "I shall make your descendants as numerous as the stars in the sky, and I will give all this Land and they shall inherit it forever." Let us say, Amen.

## The Great Protector

God who protected Daniel in the Lion's den, protected Jonah in the belly of the fish, rescued Hananiah, Mishael, and Azariah from the furnace, listened to Mordechai and Esther in Shushan, guarded Ezra in exile, who answers the oppressed, the broken hearted, the humbled of spirit, the righteous and devoted, the innocent and upright — protect Israel today and everyday. Amen.

## STOP THE EVIL PLANS

Listen to our voice, God, spare Israel! Please have compassion and show favor by listening to our prayers: Stop those who plot evil against Israel, who prepare missiles and rockets to terrorize the innocent. Thwart their plans, dash their designs against earth, and pay them back in kind. Do not desert Israel in this time of need. Give us a sign of good things, and may those who hate Israel be shamed. May the words of my mouth, and thoughts in our hearts find favor with You. Amen.

## Guardian of Israel

Guardian of Israel, guard the people of Israel and don't allow Israel to perish. Protect all who declare their love for You.

Guardian of Israel the holy nation, guard them, and don't let this nation, who proclaim your unity, be destroyed.

God, You are satisfied by calls for compassion, be conciliatory toward Israel and this land, for only in You do we trust.

Creator of the universe, be gracious and answer our prayers, though we have so few worthy deeds. Act with charity and loving-kindness, and save the nation of Israel. Amen.

# Prayer for Israel's Soldiers

God who blessed our ancestors, Abraham, Isaac and Jacob, Sarah, Rebecca, Leah and Rachel, bless the members of the Israel Defense Forces and its security services who stand guard over the land and the cities of God, from the Lebanese border to the Egyptian desert, and from the Mediterranean Sea to the approach of the Aravah, and wherever else they are, on land, in air, and on the sea. Make the enemies who rise up against Israel's soldiers be struck down before their. Protect and deliver Israel's soldiers from all trouble and distress, affliction and illness, and send blessing and success to all the work of their hands. Subdue our enemies under them and drown them with deliverance and victory. Fulfill the verse, "It is the lord Your God who goes with you to fight for you against Your enemies, to deliver you." And let us say, Amen.[19]

## Prayers for Soldiers in Captivity

God who blessed Abraham, Isaac and Jacob, Sarah, Rebecca, Leah and Rachel, bless, protect and guard the members of Israel's Defense Forces missing in action or held captive, and other captives among Israel and it's allies, who are in distress or captivity, as we, members of a holy congregation, pray on their behalf. Show them compassion and bring them out from darkness and the shadow of death; break their bonds, deliver them from their distress, and bring them swiftly back to their families embrace. Give thanks to God for loving-kindness and for the wonders done for us; and we will fulfill the verse, "Those redeemed by God will return; they will enter Zion with singing, and everlasting joy will crown their heads. Gladness and joy will overtake them, and worry and sighing will flee away." And let us say, Amen.[20]

# CHAPTER THREE

## Psalm 144

By David. Blessed be the Lord, my Rock, Who trains my hands for battle and my fingers for war. My source of kindness and my fortress, my high tower and my rescuer, my shield, in whom I take refuge; it is God Who subdues my people under me. O Lord, what is man that You know him, that you reckon with him? A person is like a breath; our days are like a passing shadow. O Lord, incline Your heavens and descend; touch the mountains and they will smoke. Flash one bolt of lightning and You will scatter them; send out Your arrows and You will confound them. Stretch forth Your hands from on high, rescue me and deliver me from many waters, from the hand of strangers. Whose mouth speaks deceit and whose right hand is a right hand of falsehood. God, I will sing a new song to You, on a ten-stringed lyre I will sing praises to you. God who gives victory to kings, will rescue David, God's servant, from the evil sword. Rescue me and deliver me from the hand of strangers, whose mouth speaks deceit and whose right hand is a right hand of falsehood. For our sons are like plants, well grown in their youth; our daughters are like cornerstones, crafted to the shape of a palace. Our storehouses are full, overflowing with all manner of food; our flocks number thousands, growing by the tens of thousands in our open fields. Our leaders bear the heaviest burden; there is no breach, nor is there bad report, and no outcry in our streets. Happy is the people who have it so, happy is the people whose God is the Lord.[21]

# CHAPTER 4

# DAILY PSALMS FOR ISRAEL

> *"The Guardian who keeps Israel will neither slumber nor sleep."*
>
> —PSALM 121

*Rabbi Bachyeh Ben Asher, the 14th century Spanish-born scholar, wrote that if we recite Tehillim every day in honor of another Jew or for the safety of Israel, it serves to arouse God to immediately show mercy in a miraculous manner.[22] Consequently, the following five psalms are said each day for Israel: 20, 83, 121, 130, and 142. These prayers were normally reserved for times of great crisis and peril. Israel today stands in the face of annihilation from enemies, as well a enduring threats from every direction. Therefore these psalms are included in the daily prayers for Israel, as Israel needs protection now more than ever.*

## Psalm 20

For the Conductor of the universe, a psalm by David. May the Creator answer you on your day of danger; may the Name of the God of Jacob make you strong. May God send your help from the Sanctuary, and send you support from Zion. May God remember all your grain offerings, and accept your sacrifices, selah! May God grant you according to your heart and fulfill the strivings of your heart. May we shout for joy in your deliverance, and raise our banners in the name of our God; may the Creator fulfill all your wishes. Now I know that the Creator sends deliverance of victory to God's anointed; answering from God's holy heavens with mighty acts of deliverance of God's right hand. Some trust in chariots and some upon horses, but we will call on the Name of the Creator our God. Our enemies have knelt down, become weak and have been destroyed, but we have risen and stand upright. Delivers us, Oh God! Our Sovereign O, our Creator, answer us on the day we call.[23]

## Chapter Four

## Psalm 83

A song, a psalm by Asaph. O God, do not be silent; do not be at still, O God. See how Your enemies are in uproar, and those who hate You have raised their heads. They plot secretly against Your people, and conspire against those You shelter. They say, "Come, let us sever them from nationhood, and the name of Israel will be forgotten." For they conspire with a united heart, and made a covenant against You. The nations of Edom and the Ishmaelites, Moab and the Hagrites, Geval and Ammon, and Amalek, Philistia with the inhabitants of Tyre scheme together against us. Assyria, too, joined with them, and became powerful support for the sons of Lot, Selah. Destroy them as You did Midian, and Sisera and Yavin at the brook of Kishon. They were destroyed at Ein Dor, and were as dung for the earth. Make their nobles like Orev and Ze'ev, all their princes like Zevach and Tzalmuna, who said, "Let us inherit the dwellings of God for ourselves." My God, make them like whirling chaff, like straw that bends before the wind. As a fire consumes the forest, and a flame sets the mountains ablaze, so pursue them with Your tempest and frighten them with Your storm. Fill their faces with shame, that they may seek Your Name, O Lord. Let them be ashamed and terrified forever; let them be humiliated and perish. They will know that You, Whose Name is the Lord, are alone the true ruler over all the Earth.[24]

# Chapter Four

# Psalm 121

A song of ascents. I lift my eyes to the mountains, and ask where will my help come from? My help will come from the Lord, Maker of Heaven and Earth. God will not let your foot falter; your Guardian does not slumber. Indeed, the Guardian of Israel neither slumbers nor sleeps. God is your Guardian; the God is your protective shade at your right hand. The sun will not harm you by day, nor the moon by night. God will guard you from all evil; God will guard your soul. God will guard your going out and coming from this time and forever.[25]

## Psalm 130

A song of ascents. God, out of the depths I call to You. My Creator, listen to my voice; let Your ears be attentive to the sound of my pleas. God, if You were to preserve iniquities, who could survive? But forgiveness is with You, that You may be held in awe. I hope in God; my soul hopes, and I long for His word. My soul yearns for the Creator more than those awaiting the morning wait for the morning. Israel, put your hope in the Lord, for with the Creator there is kindness; with God there is abounding deliverance. And God will redeem Israel from all its iniquities.[26]

## Psalm 142

A poem written by David, when he was in the cave, as a prayer. With my voice I will cry out to the Ruler; with my voice I will call out in supplication. I will pour out my plea before God; I will declare my distress in God's presence. When my spirit is faint within me, You know my path. In the way in which I walk, they have hidden a snare for me. Look to my right and see, there is none that will know me; every escape is lost to me. No man cares for my soul. I cried out to You, O Creator; I said, "You are my refuge, my portion in the land of the living." Listen to my song of prayer, for I have been brought very low. Deliver me from my pursuers, for they are too mighty for me. Release my soul from confinement, so that it may acknowledge Your Name. When I am released through your grace, the righteous will crown You.[27]

## CHAPTER 5

## MEDITATIONS

*"You must believe that God listens and pays attention to every word of prayer, so that not a single word is lost."*

— REBBE NACHMAN

## CHAPTER FIVE

*In our prayers and thoughts about Israel we hope and pray for a complete redemption; for the ingathering of the exiles to the Promised Land; for a new light to shine on Zion — the messianic light which will radiate over Jerusalem; and for the rebuilding of the Temple in a spiritual and physical sense. "Thus is the redemption of Israel," said Rabbi Chiya the Great as he saw the sun rising over the Arabel Valley, "It begins very slowly."* [28]

*The following meditations are based on the personal prayers of Rabbi Nosson, the primary conduit for the teachings of Rebbe Nachman of Breslov. Rabbi Noson composed a lengthy book of prayers, Le'kutei Teffilot, that speak directly from the heart and address G-d as one might address a friend.*

## Hear My Prayers

God, please take pity on Your own great and holy honor. Please elevate Israel's grace and spirit, and increase our devotion to You. Have pity on Israel and those who love Israel, hear and receive our prayers, our cries, our devotion now and always. Do you see our plight? Do you see what is going on? All we ask it that You keep Your word, "God doesn't hate or spurn the suffering of the downtrodden". That is us God. That is me God. As long as Israel suffers, we are downtrodden. Please don't hide Yourself from us. When we cry out to You, with tears in our heart, please hear our prayers. God, show us favor now, and always and answer our prayers. I know that You hear the prayers of everyone with compassion. I know that You hear the prayers for Israel with love. God, hear my prayers. God, hear our prayers today.[29]

## CHAPTER FIVE

# SHOW YOUR LOVE FOR ISRAEL SO THAT WE MAY SING TO YOU

Hashem our God, God of our ancestors, who enjoys songs of praise, please listen to my prayer: Your presence is like a bird wandering from its nest, lost from home. Will you take pity on Zion? Is it not time? Hasn't Zion's time come? This is the moment. Now is the time. Israel and those who love Zion have fallen so low. Israel has lost dignity and suffered so many blows and our hearts are broken. Show Your love for Israel and for Zion so that we can raise our voices in song and praises. With our hearts full of joy, can You imagine the songs, the music, the devotion that You will hear? And please don't hold me back; give me the power and voice to praise You with music and prayers. Let me sing to You all the days of my life.[30]

## Restore Israel's Prestige

Master of the World, see our poverty, our lowliness, our shame. All of the grace and prestige of Israel has fallen in this bitter exile of 2,000 years. Israel is despised and lowly in the eyes of the nations and peoples of the world. It seems, God forbid, that Your grace and prestige have fallen to the wicked haters of Israel. How can this be? Have we gone so far astray? How much longer do we have to live with this cruel irony and shame? Please God. I beg You, please remove the aura of righteousness that rests upon those that seek to do Israel harm. Don't do it for my sake. I am asking to do it for Your sake! God — may those that seek to do Israel harm have no prestige in the world, or with You. Have compassion on the remnant of Israel, and hear these prayers.

## CHAPTER FIVE

# BRING US TO YOUR HOLY LAND

My spirit is constricted and I beseech You — please answer me with expansiveness. From the ends of the Earth, I will continue to call out to You, even as my heart is faint. Have mercy on me and help me visit Eretz Yisrael, the Holy Land, very soon. The Holy Land is the source of our holiness, as You know. All of our holiness, purity, and spiritual lives depend vitality on Eretz Yisrael. It is impossible to be a Jew — or any other believer in the Bible — to elevate us spiritually, without visiting the Holy Land, the birthplace of Holiness. This land that You choose from all the other lands of the Earth, and gave as an inheritance to the Jewish people. Israel is the land that You watch over constantly, as it is written, "A land that Hashem your God watches over continuously; from the start of the year until the end." [31]

Look at formidable obstacles — fears, wars, insecurities and distractions — which prevent me and my family from reaching the Holy Land, living in the

Holy land, or returning regularly. For 2,000 years in exile the Jewish people were prevented from returning to the source of Holiness, for they had been exiled from the Land of our ancestors. Now You have made the path wide-open. Master of the Universe! Have compassion and consideration. Place in our hearts, and the hearts of our children and the hearts of the Jewish nation, the House of Israel, the most powerful yearning, passion and desire to visit Your Holy Land, Israel. Let me, and my people, and my congregation, truly yearn and desire always to reach Israel, until You bring us there — may it be soon. Through this journey and spiritual awakening we will be more inspired to serve you. Hashem, God, I do wish to dwell in Your Holy Land, the land which is our inheritance, the rest of my days and the length of our lives.[32]

# Chapter 6

# Prayers for Jerusalem

> *"May You accept the prayer of Your servant, and of Your people Israel, when they pray toward this place."*
> — 1 KINGS 8:30

*Jerusalem is the holiest city in the world. Pilgrims still make their way there today from every corner of the Earth. This is the city where the prophets spoke, where kings ruled, and offerings and pilgrimages defined divine service. Today, visitors line the streets during Holy Days for the Jewish, Christian, Orthodox, Coptic, and Muslim faithful that call Jerusalem, and Zion, holy. Jerusalem is a city of great beauty and majesty, the home of prayer, and a gateway to heaven. The following prayers can be recited on Jerusalem Day, or any other day. We pray that peace will reign in Jerusalem until the final redemption.*

## SERVICE OF THE HEART

Fill my heart with awe and fear of God so that these prayers emanate from my heart. Let me recognize the virtue of Israel, so that I may pray genuinely for its redemption. Let me recognize the virtues of the Holy Land, its qualities, its sanctity, so that I pray from the depths of my heart for the rebuilding of Jerusalem.[33]

## Beauty

Fill the world with the radiance of Jerusalem, the blessed city. As the ancient sages wrote, "Ten measures of beauty came down to Earth: nine were taken by Jerusalem and one by the rest of the world (Kiddushin 49b)." Let the beauty of Jerusalem shine forth as a beacon of light and illumination in the darkness.

## CHAPTER SIX

# Psalm 122

A song of pilgrimage by David: I rejoiced when they said, "Let us go up to God's House." Our feet would stand within your gates, Jerusalem. The City of Jerusalem is built to bring unity, because it is there that the tribes ascend to serve you as one nation of God, a testimony to Israel, to praise Your name in Your house. For it is there that seats of justice are set, thrones of the house of David. Pray for the peace of Jerusalem, where those who love you be tranquil. Peace be within Your walls, serenity in your palaces. For the sake of my brothers and friends I say, peace be with you." This is the house of God the Almighty, I seek the best for you.

## Blessed is Jerusalem the Home of Prayer

Thank you God for the liberation of Jerusalem, and the great day on which the blessed Rock of Israel, favored us to come to this pleasant land and see with our eyes the beginning of the flourishing of the redemption of Israel.[34] God, I know that the elevation of all prayers is bound to the sanctity of our Holy Land and the Holy City of Jerusalem, the dwelling place of holiness and the Gate of Heaven, whose transcendent nature was revealed to us by our hallowed ancestors, the prophets and divinely inspired seers. As King Solomon said at the inauguration of the Temple, "And they shall pray to You by way of their land, which You have given to their ancestors, the city which You have chosen and the house which I have built for Your name." Because our prayers today focus on the Holy Land and the Holy City, the city, which is the spiritual home for the world, the sanctity of Jerusalem elevates the inner value of every prayer that is spoken. May God bless Jerusalem, home of prayer.[35]

# NEXT YEAR IN JERUSALEM

When we sat by the waters of Babylon and wept as we recalled Zion, when our hearts were broken and our spirits depressed over the destruction of the Holy City, we swore to remember our homeland and direct ourselves towards Jerusalem. In the words of the prophet: "If I forget you, O Jerusalem, let my right hand forget its skill. If I do not remember you, let my tongue join the roof of my mouth, if I do not set Jerusalem above my highest joy." (Ps. 137:5) The voice that accompanies us with pleasant hope twice a year — on the first nights of Passover and the last prayer on Yom Kippur — is the voice of the soul expressing its deepest desire, "Next year in Jerusalem."

Next year may Jerusalem be free of war and conflict. Next year may all the world recognize the sanctity of Jerusalem. Next year may the redeemer come to Jerusalem.

Shana Ha'ba b' Yerushalyim. Next Year in Jerusalem. Amen.[36]

## Psalm 137

By the rivers of Babylon, there we sat and we wept as we remembered Zion. On willows in its midst we hung our harps. There our captors asked us words of the song, and our tormentors amused themselves saying: "Sing for us a song of Zion." How can we sing the song of our God in a strange land?

If I forget you Jerusalem, may my right hand forget its skill. May my tongue fuse to my palate, if I do not remember you, if I do not bring up Jerusalem at the beginning of my joy. Remember, Almighty, how the sons of Edom, the day of the destruction of Jerusalem, who said, "Raze it, raze it, down to its foundation!" Child of Babylon, you are destined to be destroyed and plundered because God is a God of Justice and will reward you for your evil treatment of our people, our innocents and the desecration of our holy places. You will receive an equal measure of suffering. Praised is the one who brings your dark reward. Praised is the one who enacts justice on your guilty soldiers and your innocent babes.

# CHAPTER 7

## PRAYERS FOR TIMES OF CRISIS

*"And at that time, Micha'el, will stand up, the great chief angel, who stands for the children of Your people: and there shall be a time of trouble, such as never was since there was a nation 'til that same time: and at that time your people will be delivered."*

— DANIEL 12:1

*When Israel is facing dire situations of drought, wars, and threat of wars, we have extra incentive to increase prayer. You might ask, what more can we say that we have not already said? There are certain prayers, like certain medicines, which are used as a last resort. These prayers are based on the venerable prayers said on fast days, days of great sadness, days of great trials and tribulations. Traditionally, communities would fast when faced with existential threats. While fasting can help one achieve a state of heightened God consciousness, not everyone will be able to fast. Whether you are fasting or not, these prayers echo the prayers said by those engaged in fasting, and other prayers and psalms for times of great distress.*

## Awakening God's Compassion

Compassionate and gracious God, you are slow to anger, abounding in loving-kindness and truth, extending your affection and care to a thousand generations, forgiving iniquity, rebellion and sin, and absolving those who repent. Forgive us our mistakes and our failings. Connect us to Your love as is our birthright. Forgive us God, for You are good and forgiving, abounding in loving kindness to all who call on You.

## Prayer for Captives

God of mercy, save our brothers and sisters who are captive or in danger. Save them on the land and upon the open sea, for the whole world is Yours to rule. Hear their cry and answer them, bring relief to the distressed. Redeem the oppressed and subjugated souls. Deliver those who dwell in darkness into the light of freedom and salvation. Accept our petition and save them in the blink of an eye.

# CHAPTER SEVEN

# PRAYER FOR ZION AND JERUSALEM

*The following prayer is based on a traditional prayer said on Tisha B'Av. Tisha B'Av is the saddest day of the Jewish year because of the incredible series of tragedies that occurred on that date throughout Jewish History. We mourn the destruction of both Holy Temples, people fast and refrain from any activities that are pleasurable.*

## HOW LONG MUST THERE BE WEEPING?

How long must there be weeping in Zion and eulogy in Jerusalem? Show Zion mercy and rebuild the walls of Jerusalem?[37] Show Zion mercy and establish it as You promised, hurry the salvation, and speed the redemption, and return Jerusalem with great compassion. As it is written by the hands of the Prophet: Therefore, this is what God said, "I will return to Jerusalem with compassion, I will rebuild My house there, said the Master of Legions and a measuring string will stretch over Jerusalem.[38] Over the destruction of the Temple, That was torn down and trampled, I shall lament with a new eulogy every year, for the holiness lost and the Temple.[39]

# Psalm for Great Crisis – Psalm 59

*The following Psalm is said in times of great need for Israel. In Chapter 4 are psalms that are said regularly, these particular psalms are said in times of crisis, not as preventative measures, but to make sure that Israel survives conflict as it happens.*

## Save me from my Enemies

For the Conductor of the universe, remember the letter David wrote as he saw the guards King Saul sent lying in wait and surrounding his house to kill him. Remember this and save me. I too need salvation from the enemies who rise up and surround me. Make me strong enough to fend off my attackers.

Don't let me fall into the hands of traitors, spies and bloodthirsty men. See how they plot and plan for my destruction. They oppress me without cause, and aim to reap my soul. See how they have no conscience as they prepare themselves for a war against me, and defend me.

Creator of the universe, ruler of the heavens, God of Israel do not continue to ignore the servants of evil and the enemies of justice forever. Do not grant them success, remove your grace from them and rise and rule your domain with justice. They encircle the city each night howling like wild dogs. Their mouths erupt with hatred. They wage war with words crafted and honed as sharp as swords to maim and kill us in the eyes of the nations of the world . But You know the truth and will scoff and reject their claims against us. You will answer them with scorn and mockery.

Remember David your loyal servant, and answer me as you answered him. I rely upon You my fortress and hope. You, God of kindness see all and will lead me and reveal to me the plots of those scheming against me. Take away their power and destroy their materials of destruction. Do not kill them for us because soon we will forget their evil and another will rise in their place.

Guard us, our shield and protector. Each poisonous word that pours from their lips is a sin against You. Their arrogance will bring them down and they will be imprisoned by their lies and curses. Unleash your wrath, destroy them and they will know that it is You who rule over Jacob and the lands of the Earth forever. They will return and again encircle the city each night howling like wild dogs. And like wild dogs they will scavenge to fill their bellies and roam to satisfy their hunger. They will blockade the city throughout the long night. When dawn breaks in the morning and they flee, I will sing praises of Your kindness. You are my stronghold and my refuge in the dark of night when the wild dogs howl. My strength! To You I will sing for God is my stronghold, O God of Kindness.

## CHAPTER SEVEN

# Prayers for Rain

*The Bible teaches that drought comes to the Land of Israel through idolatry, but that God can reverse this judgment in an instant; "God shall open for you His storehouse of goodness, the heavens, to provide rain for your land in its time, and to bless all your handiwork. You shall lend to many nations, but you shall not borrow." Deuteronomy 28:12*

*The Talmud [40] tells the story of a long drought in the Land of Israel. Public fasts were proclaimed and special prayers were said. The great Torah Scholar Rabbi Eliezer was called upon to lead the prayers and with the invocation of a 24 blessing prayer, which is said at times of severe drought. Despite this, no rain fell. Rabbi Eliezer's disciple, Rabbi Akiva, came to the front and said a special prayer of five lines in which each verse began with the words, Avinu Malkeinu, literally "Our Father, Our King" to awaken God's compassion and sympathy. After he finished the rain fell. Over the years many other verses have been added. This prayer below is based on the Avinu Malkinu said during fast days and daily during the Ten Days of Repentance from Rosh Hashanah to Yom Kippur. The prayers here have been modified to focus on Israel's national needs and repentance.*

*Let us pray that our sins be overlooked, that our transgressions be pardoned, and that Israel will be spared more hardship.*

## Creator of the Universe Answer our Prayers

God, we have sinned before you. We have no other ruler but you. Nullify all harsh decrees upon Israel. Nullify the plans of those who hate Israel. Thwart the counsel of our enemies. Wipe out every foe and adversary of Israel. Seal the mouths of our adversaries and accusers. Remove famine, bloodshed, and destruction. Remove hostility to Your covenant with Israel. Forgive Israel's sins and pardon all transgressions. Return Israel to You in repentance. Send complete recovery to the sick of Israel. Tear up the evil decree of Israel's verdict. Remember

Israel for life. Remember Israel for redemption and salvation. Remember Israel for forgiveness. Make salvation sprout blossom for us soon. Raise high the dignity of Israel. Fill Israel's hands with blessing. Open the Gates of Heaven to our prayers. Decree this a moment of compassion and a time of favor. Take pity on Israel, and upon Israel's children. Avenge the spilled blood of Your servants. Act for Your sake, if not for Israel's sake. God, our Creator, be gracious with Israel, answer our prayers, though we have few worthy deeds, and treat us with charity and kindness, and save Israel.

## Answer Us — A Prayer for Rain

Answer us, Creator of the world, with Your attribute of mercy. God who chooses the nation Israel to make known Your greatness and glory. God who hears prayers – grant dew and rain to the face of the earth and satiate the whole world from Your goodness and grace. Fill our hands from Your blessing and from the wealth of Your giving Hand. Protect and save Israel this year from anything evil, from any type of disaster, from any type of tragedy and provide Israel this year with hope and peace. Have mercy upon us with the blessing of rain for Israel's fields, orchards, vineyards and gardens, so they will blossom and sustain Israel's inhabitants. We want Israel to be worthy of a life of plenty and peace again. May Israel merit a life of plenty and peace as in the good years; and remove eradicate all pestilence, sickness, famine, wild animals, slavery, plunder and illness. Prevent disaster from damaging the land and bringing pain and suffering to Israel's homes. Banish from our hearts the cunning of the evil inclination that leads us astray. Judge Israel mercifully, and the quality of mercy will triumph over all harsh decrees. Lead Israel mercifully so that Israel too may be merciful. Accept this heartfelt repentance, remove this punishment, and save Israel from destruction.[41]

# About This Book

*"You must pray for everything."*

— REBBE NACHMAN OF BRESLOV[42]

## ABOUT THIS BOOK

As a Fulbright fellow in Krakow, Poland, in 1993, I prayed weekly in a five hundred year-old synagogue in what had been the old Jewish ghetto. The walls were painted with frescos of Rachel's Tomb and The Western Wall, places where Jews have prayed for millennia. The frescoes inspired the members of the congregation to not just pray, but to keep Israel in their prayers. They prayed for the redemption of Israel, the ingathering of the exiles and an era of peace over Jerusalem. As a young graduate student the frescos reminded me of the eternal connection between the Jewish people and the Holy Land. The pre-war Polish Jewish civilization was destroyed in the Holocaust, but the longing for Zion, the love of Israel, and the fervent prayers at our holy sites remain.

I began compiling prayers about Israel after serving as Campus Rabbi at America's most virulently anti-Israel university, where speaker after speaker called for Israel's destruction. Searching for prayers for and about Israel, I discovered that while these prayers are very powerful, they are often in Hebrew or in an English style that no one speaks. Consequently the prayers are inaccessible to most readers. The prayers are generally terse and compact to conserve space or to be memorized, or written poetically in order to be chanted. As a result, these beloved prayers are beyond the grasp of the average parishioner. The deeply embedded meaning, faith and wisdom of the ancient sages them escape us. So too, many of the Psalms that we recite today for Israel in crisis are not translated in a way that makes them comfortable to recite on a regular basis. The "thous", and "arts", disguise the beauty of the ancient words for the contemporary reader.

I realized that to wage a serious spiritual battle prayers were needed that could be recited without the distractions of antiquated language. Also more prayers were needed that dealt with the current situation. Prayers that give voice to both the ancient and the modern and express our deepest yearnings. So I began to transcribe existing prayers, to collect meditations and writings, and finally began to write down my own personal prayers for Israel and for peace.

## ABOUT THIS BOOK

*Prayers for Israel* originates from a belief I share with millions of people that the power of prayer can help bring peace to Israel and the Middle East. We can pray alone, in small groups or at rallies in the spiritual struggle for peace. As conflicts on Israel's borders are increasing, and nations and groups rally to the call for Israel's destruction, we need to strengthen ourselves. Our spiritual devotion and yearning for a peaceful resolution to the conflict is powerful. Prayers concerning Israel's safety and wellbeing can and should be part of the worldwide campaign to legitimize, protect, and defend Israel from its enemies.

As Rabbi Shlomo Carlebach taught, "Our prayers are reflected by the way we live. Prayer is not overcoming God's reluctance, but taking hold of God's willingness. Courage is fear that has said its prayers."

# How To Use This Book

*"Your main weapon is prayer. You may have to fight many battles, both with the Evil Urge and with many things that prevent you from serving God. With prayer you conquer them all."*

— REBBE NACHMAN OF BRESLOV

## HOW TO USE THIS BOOK

God teaches us that if we remember Israel and Jerusalem each day we will hasten the return of the Messiah to the Holy City. We are intrinsically connected to Israel and Jerusalem. As it says in Psalm 137, "If I forget you Jerusalem, may my right hand forget its skill." This book can help you keep Israel and Jerusalem close to your heart and prayers.

The prayers you have in your hands will keep open the lines of communication with God, focus your thoughts and prayers on Israel, and connect you with those who pray for Israel the world over. Whether you use this book everyday, or only when the spirit moves you, you'll find prayers that come from the heart, written or inspired by our holy sages, poets and prophets. Our prayers and our meditations will beseech God that we no longer want to live in a world where is Israel is threatened but a world where Israel is at peace. This peace will radiate through the world bringing peace between brothers and sisters, between families, between all nations and people as we approach the final redemption.

The book begins with answering the questions about the holiness of the land of Israel. Why is Israel, well, Israel? What makes it so special? Why in the world do we pray for Israel? We can't loose sight of why we are praying for Israel for a moment. With the onslaught of negativity that reaches you at home, in your office, on your smartphone, we can become ambivalent. Yet, ambivalence is not an option now. Nothing about the existence of the State of Israel is an accident, and the continued existence of the state is of great spiritual importance. Read about "The Holiness of Israel" whenever the forces of hate reach you.

The following chapters contain prayers are composed to be recited on a regular basis. Read one or some, read them when waiting in line or on hold, or as part of your daily personal prayers to God. We begin with a prayer inspired by *Shema Yisrael*, proclaiming the unity and oneness of God. This central tenet of the Bible reminds us that everything ultimately emanates from God, and that to God alone do we direct our prayers. This is followed by a selection of prayers inspired by the standing daily prayer, the *Amidah*, which is part of daily Jewish devotion and prayer. These prayers are written in the plural because they speak on behalf of all lovers of Israel. While some points may not apply to you personally, they do apply to someone in the family of those who love Israel. These include prayers asking God for salvation, for protection, the ingathering of the exiles, defeating Israel's enemies, prayers for the righteous, rebuilding Jerusalem, the State of Israel, and the coming of the Messiah.

Following this we ask God to hear our prayers. We might think, "Who am I that God will listen to my prayers? I'm a simple person, I'm an imperfect person, why does God want to hear from me?" However, is there a parent that does not want to hear the voice of their child? It doesn't matter the circumstances, but when a child calls out to their parent, the parent should stop their activity and listen, because that is how deep the love of a parent is for a child. God too wants to hear from each of us, and have us call out as assuredly as a child who trusts that a parent will always answer.

Next we thank God. Why does God need our thanks? Why would the Master of the world, the Creator, need affirmation from me? We know that a prayer of thanks to God is like an offering. In the days of the Holy Temple the Israelites showed appreciation for all that God did for them with thanksgiving offerings. Today there is no Temple, and there are no physical offerings, and what remains are the prayers and the songs of thanks and praise. We thank God for all that we have. We thank God for the miracles that sustain us each day and make it possible to serve God. The regular practice of prayer allows us to develop our abilities to see blessings in our lives. As our strength in prayer grows so does our appreciation to the Creator. This builds our faith and strengthens our love and awe of God.

After we thank God for everything, we include a prayer for peace, because peace is the greatest blessing of all. You can have your health, you can have wealth, but if you lack peace, or are living in fear, you have no rest.

We have thanked God, we have prayed for so many things, and we have asked God to hear our prayers — but now we pray that God accept our prayers. Our prayers should not be in vain, but accepted by the Creator of the universe.

In order to hasten the acceptance of our personal prayers we pray for a refinement of our character. Each of us has the capacity to be a righteous person. We ask God to help us guard our tongue, be open to wisdom and other people, remove anger, develop humility and awe, nullify our inner demons, and then we ask that our prayers from the heart be accepted.

**Chapter Three** contains daily prayers for Israel's protection. We ask God to shelter Israel and protect its citizens from enemies and attacks. We pray for those brave people who risk their lives to ensure security for Israel. Additionally we pray for all defenders of Israel. While some of these prayers are traditionally said in a group on the Sabbath, they can be recited anytime.

The power to draw down the indwelling presence of God is strongest in-group prayer. An intentional prayer community retains a measure of spiritual gravity that was experienced in the Temple, and some prayers are traditionally reserved in the Jewish tradition exclusively for community prayer.

**Chapter Four** contains daily Psalms of King David considered very auspicious to say during times of crisis. These five psalms embody our prayers that Israel be saved from its enemies, and that Israel make amends with God. There are many people that recite them every single day. With nuclear threats from Iran and worldwide boycotts of Israeli goods, culture, and people, I include them as something we can add to strengthen our daily prayers.

**Chapter Five** contains prayers and meditations from one of greatest teachers of prayer, the holy Rebbe Nachman of Breslov. His prayers are unique as they speak from the heart. They can be said any day or at any moment in any place when you feel that you need to connect to God on a deep and personal level. These prayers, based on his teachings, are translations of prayers authored by his student Rebbe Nosson. They were made available to the public in a usable way thanks to the Breslov Research Institute. I made a few of my own insertions in this chapter as well.

**Chapter Six** focuses entirely on Jerusalem, the eternal capital of Israel. Jerusalem is central to the religious convictions of many faiths. It is a center of devotion and ritual for many people. The name has been translated as "The City of Peace." Sadly today and throughout history, this city has been the center of struggles and bloodshed. The Jewish people pray towards Jerusalem, pilgrims of all faiths visit the Holy City and experience what our sages call the place 'where Heaven meets Earth.' There is a tradition, which even says that all the world's prayers travel to God via Jerusalem. Jerusalem is also the focus of our prayers during times of great travail and during moments of joy. Jerusalem is a place on the globe, but equally it signifies the world of spirituality. A person can feel a connection to the divine in Jerusalem that exists uniquely there.

**Chapter Seven** is for crisis. From drought to warfare, these are moments when Israel's very existence is at stake. When rains cease to fall Israel is in serious danger. Enough rain is always a sign of God's blessing, and drought or deluge signifies that we have taken steps away from God. Even now, as Israel is enjoying an explosion of creativity, production and technology innovation, no one but God can regulate the rain. All we can do is manage what has fallen. With one reservoir, the Sea of Galilee, and a growing population, water plays a central role in Israel's well being. We pray that the rains fall and when they don't, that Israel redirects its focus and comes closer to God, closer to peace between sisters and brothers and the nations of the world.

When the missiles rain down, and bombs are exploding like thunder and striking like lightning, it is instinctive to pray because Israel is in serious crisis. Just as frightened children cling to their parents when the air-raid sirens blare, so too we should reach out to God for protection and comfort. Fervent payers said "in a fox-hole" are heard for sure and these there impassioned please are powerful.. But when we are searching for passion in our daily prayers we turn to the poets, the psalmists and the prayer book to strengthen our practice and to let us voice our deepest concerns.

Keep *Prayers for Israel* in a convenient location. When you have a moment as you wait in line, or are on hold, you will be amazed how many prayers you can say. Say these prayers in addition to your daily prayers. As you recite them, they will become more familiar and your recitation more eloquent. Remember that many of these prayers are based on the compositions of the sages. They wrote them to help us express in words, what we feel, when our own words are blocked and fail us. **God bless you for your praying for Israel.**

# BIBLIOGRAPHY

Carlebach, Rabbi Shlomo, *Am Yisrael Chai, Israel is Living: Teachings and Stories,* privately published by his students.

Donin, Rabbi Hayim Halevy, *To Pray as a Jew: A Guide to the Prayer Book and the Synagogue Service,* Basic Books, New York 1980.

Feuer, Rabbi Avrohom Chaim, *Shemoneh Esrei, The Amidah/The Eighteen Blessings,* Mesorah Publications, New York 1999.

Kaplan, Aryeh, Jerusalem: *Eye of the Universe,* National Conference of Synagogue Youth, Mesorah Publications, 1976.

Greenbaum, Avraham, Trans. *The Fiftieth Gate, Lekutei Tefilot, Reb Nosson's Prayers,* Breslov Research Institute, Vol. 1-2, Jerusalem/New York, 1992

Neriyah, Rabbi Moshe Zvi, *Celebration of the Soul: The Holidays in the Life and Thought of Rabbi Avraham Yitzchak Kook,* Trans. Jaffe, Pesach, Genesis Jerusalem Press, Jerusalem 1992.

Ritchie, Zvi, *Rebbe Nachman Says...The Teachings of Rabbi Nachman of Breslov as Taught by Rabbi Shlomo Carlebach,* 2011.

Sachs, Rabbi Sir Jonathan Sacks, *The Koren Siddur, American Edition,* Koren Publishers, Jerusalem 2009.

Steinsaltz, Rabbi Adin, *A Guide to Jewish Prayer*, Schoken Books, New York, 2000.

Yerushalmi, Rabbi Shmuel, *The Book of Tehillim, Me'am Lo'ez, Vol. 1-5*, trans. Dr. Zvi Faier, Moznaim Publishing, New York 1991.

# ENDNOTES

# ENDNOTES

[01] Lamed Vav

[02] Rav Kook, Igrot 1, quoted in Neriyah Pg. 183

[03] Quoted in Rabbi Avraham Aryeh Trugman's "Holiness and the Land of Israel".

[04] Based on the central tenet of Jewish belief, the oneness of God, *Sh'ma Yisrael Adonai Eloheinu, Adonai Echad.*

[05] This meditation is based on the seventh blessing of the Amida, is a "plea for personal triumph over adversity," (Feuer:122). We ask God to help us bear the burdens of life, and the adversity that we are faced with each day so we may dedicate ourselves to Israel's safety.

[06] This prayer is based on the tenth prayer of the Amidah. This is a plea for the redemption of the entire Jewish nation who cannot be truly free while in Exile. The redemption will begin, only once all of the Jewish people will be gathered together and reunited. [Hirsch:138] Rabbi Abba taught in the Talmud, Sanhedrin 98a, that there is no more obvious sign of the final redemption that the flowering of Israel's hills. If the land ceases mourning, it is because her children are coming home. [Feuer:154]

[07] This prayer is based on the 12th prayer of the Amidah. Today, some of the greatest detractors are themselves people who grew up in a Jewish home, but turned against Israel.

[08] This prayer is based on the thirteenth prayer of the Amidah. This prayer encouraged those that are facing adversity in their holy lives, to not be discouraged by misfortunes. As it is written in Psalm 75:11, *All the pride of the wicked I shall cut down; exalted shall be the pride of the righteous.* [Feuer:190]

[09] This prayer is based on the fourteenth prayer of the Amidah. Jerusalem was a beacon of spiritual light that is now dimmed because of the destruction of the Temple. We pray that the city be rebuilt so the light of Jerusalem can illuminate the world. The name Jerusalem is a contraction of the Hebrew words for fear of heaven, and peace and harmony and peoples, representing spiritual and communal aspirations. (Feuer p. 202, quoting commentary of Rabbi Yehuda ben Yakar on the Midrash.)

[10] Based on Sacks, p. 522.

[11] Based on the fifteenth blessing of the Amidah. The coming of the Messiah is related to Israel's deeds.

There is an appointed time for the Messiah, but this time can be hastened. As it says in the Talmud, "If they are deserving I will hasten it. If they are not, it will be in its appointed time." (Sanhedrin 98a)

[12] Isaiah 51:3

[13] Isaiah 11:1,2

[14] Based on the nineteenth prayer of the Amidah which is a general prayer for our needs. After praying for many things, we ask god for our personal needs and that our prayers be accepted. It is customary to include their personal prayers in this blessing.

[15] Isaiah 56:7 quoted in Feuer p. 224

[16] Based on the nineteenth blessing of the Amidah. The concluding prayer is a request for peace. Peace is the ultimate blessing. You can have wealth, good health, food and drink, but if you have no peace it's worthless. (Based on Sifra and Feuer)

[17] Based on the concluding prayer of the Amidah. As it says in Psalms, "My Lord, open my lips that my mouth may declare Your praise (Psalm 51:17) We ask God that we use our power of speech for good, for prayer, for advocacy and to represent those that don't have

a voice. Judah ben Samuel's 12th century work, Sefer Chareidim, teaches that this prayer is a constant prayer that we might be saved from our own evil inclinations which threaten us and our relationship with God.

[18] From the Morning Service

[19] From The Koren Siddur, translation by Rabbi Sir Jonathan Sacks, Jerusalem 2009, p. 524.

[20] Based on Sacks, p. 524.

[21] David is thankful to God for having given him the strength to wage war against his enemies. He mentions his battle with Goliath in verse 2, and thanks God for making him the victor

[22] MeAm Loez, Vol. 3

[23] This psalm was chanted by King David every time he dispatched Joab to lead the Jewish people into battle and is a prayer on their behalf. If a loved one or relative is suffering — *even in a distant place, where one is unable to help — offer this prayer on their behalf.*

[24] Asaph composed this psalm about all the places in exile where the Jewish people would be in the future. The psalm closes by making it clear that those nations who

marched against Israel will suffer the consequences.

[25] This is a psalm of consolation. The Singer compares the exile to a man travelling on the road who is waylaid by bandits: they want to kill him and rob him. He raises his eyes to the mountains, looking for someone to hear his appeal and come to his assistance. The sages also explain, " I lift up my eyes to the mountains" — to the King Messiah. Thus it is written, "Who are you O great mountain?" (Zacharia 4:7). From where will he come? By way of the mountains! As it says, "How beautiful upon the mountains are the feet of the one who brings good tidings" (Isaiah 52:7). This psalm alludes to the Lower Paradise, from which one ascends to the Higher Paradise. It also speaks of how God watches over us. (Meam Loez)

[26] David composed this psalm about himself, but intended for the future exiles. They should conduct themselves as he did and then God will have mercy upon them.

[27] David composed this psalm while hiding from Saul in a cave, at which time he had cut off the corner of Saul's garment (to prove that he was able to kill him

but did not wish to do so). He prayed to God to bring him out of the cave safely. He declared, "Where can I turn, and where can I run? All I have is to cry out to You!"

[28] From the Palestinian Talmud Berachot 1:1, and Yoma 3:2, quoted in Neriya p. 183.

[29] Based on Lekutei Tefillos 1

[30] ibid:3

[31] ibid:20.

[32] ibid:20.

[33] Based on *Musar Avicha* pp.19-20 quoted in Neriyah pp. 217-8.

[34] Rav Kook to his son in *Igrot II*, pp. 292, quoted in Neriyah, p. 215

[35] This prayer is based on *Ma'amarei HaReiyah* pp. 302-3, quoted in Neriyah pp. 216-7.

[36] As appears in the Passover Haggadah

[37] From Kinot 5.

[38] Zacharia 1:16

[39] Kinot 24

[40] Taanis

[41] This prayer, mentioned in the Talmudic Tractate of Taanit, is traditionally said during Shacharit (Morning Prayers) in the Shemona Esrei (Silent Prayer), in the blessing of Shma Koleinu (Hear Our Prayers)

[42] Sichot HaRan

# PRAYERS FOR ISRAEL

# About the Author

Rabbi Yonah Bookstein is a lifelong Zionist with over twenty years of experience advocating for Israel in North American and Europe. Rabbi Yonah was ordained by Ohr Somayach Yeshiva in Monsey New York under the tutelage of the current Gateshead Rav Rabbi Shraga Feivel Zimmerman. He holds Masters Degree in Jewish Studies from Oxford University and completed a Fulbright Fellowship on post-war, Polish-Jewish relations at Jagiellonian University in Krakow. During the 1990's as director of the Ronald S. Lauder Foundation in Poland, he spearheaded efforts at Jewish community renewal. In the United States he has achieved national recognition as a grassroots organizer of Jewish students defending Israel on America's most notoriously anti-Israel campuses. In 2009 he was named a Jewish Community Hero by the Jewish Federations of North

America and listed in the Forward's 50 most influential Jews in North America. Rabbi Yonah has been named the #1 Rabbi on Twitter and maintains a large social media imprint which earned him the accolade as one of the ten most influential Jews in Social Media in 2012. He publishes regularly on HuffingtonPost.com, JewishJournal.com, and Jewlicious.com. Rabbi Yonah lives in Los Angeles, with his wife Rachel and four children.

Made in the USA
Coppell, TX
19 May 2022